WEEK OF:									
GOALS:									
TOPIC	DESCRIPTION	Su							
CHORDS									
SCALES									
ARPEGGIOS									
SONGS									
LICKS/RIFFS									
OTHER									

T
A
B

T
A
B

WEEK OF:									
GOALS:			MINUTES						
TOPIC	DESCRIPTION		Sun	Mon	Tue	Wed	Thu	Fri	Sat
CHORDS									
SCALES									
ARPEGGIOS									
SONGS									
LICKS/RIFFS									
OTHER									

WEEK OF:		MINUTES						
GOALS:								
TOPIC	DESCRIPTION	Sun	Mon	Tue	Wed	Thu	Fri	Sat
CHORDS								
SCALES								
ARPEGGIOS								
SONGS								
LICKS/RIFFS								
OTHER								

WEEK OF:									
GOALS:			MINUTES						
TOPIC	DESCRIPTION		Sun	Mon	Tue	Wed	Thu	Fri	Sat
CHORDS									
SCALES									
ARPEGGIOS									
SONGS									
LICKS/RIFFS									
OTHER									

WEEK OF:								
GOALS:		MINUTES						
TOPIC	DESCRIPTION	Sun	Mon	Tue	Wed	Thu	Fri	Sat
CHORDS								
SCALES								
ARPEGGIOS								
SONGS								
LICKS/RIFFS								
OTHER								

WEEK OF:									
GOALS:		MINUTES							
TOPIC	DESCRIPTION	Sun	Mon	Tue	Wed	Thu	Fri	Sat	
CHORDS									
SCALES									
ARPEGGIOS									
SONGS									
LICKS/RIFFS									
OTHER									

T
A
B

T
A
B

WEEK OF:				MINUTES						
GOALS:										
TOPIC	DESCRIPTION		Sun	Mon	Tue	Wed	Thu	Fri	Sat	
CHORDS										
SCALES										
ARPEGGIOS										
SONGS										
LICKS/RIFFS										
OTHER										

WEEK OF:									
GOALS:			MINUTES						
TOPIC	DESCRIPTION		Sun	Mon	Tue	Wed	Thu	Fri	Sat
CHORDS									
SCALES									
ARPEGGIOS									
SONGS									
LICKS/RIFFS									
OTHER									

WEEK OF:									
GOALS:		MINUTES							
TOPIC	DESCRIPTION	Sun	Mon	Tue	Wed	Thu	Fri	Sat
CHORDS								
SCALES								
ARPEGGIOS								
SONGS								
LICKS/RIFFS								
OTHER								

WEEK OF:									
GOALS:			**MINUTES**						
TOPIC	**DESCRIPTION**		Sun	Mon	Tue	Wed	Thu	Fri	Sat
CHORDS									
SCALES									
ARPEGGIOS									
SONGS									
LICKS/RIFFS									
OTHER									

T
A
B

T
A
B

WEEK OF:								
GOALS:		MINUTES						
TOPIC	DESCRIPTION	Sun	Mon	Tue	Wed	Thu	Fri	Sat
CHORDS								
SCALES								
ARPEGGIOS								
SONGS								
LICKS/RIFFS								
OTHER								

WEEK OF:									
GOALS:				MINUTES					
TOPIC	DESCRIPTION		Sun	Mon	Tue	Wed	Thu	Fri	Sat
CHORDS									
SCALES									
ARPEGGIOS									
SONGS									
LICKS/RIFFS									
OTHER									

T
A
B

T
A
B

WEEK OF:									
GOALS:			MINUTES						
TOPIC	DESCRIPTION		Sun	Mon	Tue	Wed	Thu	Fri	Sat
CHORDS									
SCALES									
ARPEGGIOS									
SONGS									
LICKS/RIFFS									
OTHER									

WEEK OF:								
GOALS:		MINUTES						
TOPIC	DESCRIPTION	Sun	Mon	Tue	Wed	Thu	Fri	Sat
CHORDS								
SCALES								
ARPEGGIOS								
SONGS								
LICKS/RIFFS								
OTHER								

WEEK OF:								
GOALS:		MINUTES						
TOPIC	DESCRIPTION	Sun	Mon	Tue	Wed	Thu	Fri	Sat
CHORDS								
SCALES								
ARPEGGIOS								
SONGS								
LICKS/RIFFS								
OTHER								

WEEK OF:								
GOALS:		MINUTES						
TOPIC	DESCRIPTION	Sun	Mon	Tue	Wed	Thu	Fri	Sat
CHORDS								
SCALES								
ARPEGGIOS								
SONGS								
LICKS/RIFFS								
OTHER								

WEEK OF:									
GOALS:		MINUTES							
TOPIC	DESCRIPTION	Sun	Mon	Tue	Wed	Thu	Fri	Sat
CHORDS								
SCALES								
ARPEGGIOS								
SONGS								
LICKS/RIFFS								
OTHER								

WEEK OF:									
GOALS:									
TOPIC	**DESCRIPTION**				**MINUTES**				
		Sun	Mon	Tue	Wed	Thu	Fri	Sat	
CHORDS									
SCALES									
ARPEGGIOS									
SONGS									
LICKS/RIFFS									
OTHER									

T
A
B

T
A
B

WEEK OF:		MINUTES							
GOALS:		Sun	Mon	Tue	Wed	Thu	Fri	Sat
TOPIC	DESCRIPTION							
CHORDS								
SCALES								
ARPEGGIOS								
SONGS								
LICKS/RIFFS								
OTHER								

WEEK OF:								
GOALS:				MINUTES				
TOPIC	DESCRIPTION	Sun	Mon	Tue	Wed	Thu	Fri	Sat
CHORDS								
SCALES								
ARPEGGIOS								
SONGS								
LICKS/RIFFS								
OTHER								

T
A
B

T
A
B

WEEK OF:							
GOALS:		MINUTES					
TOPIC	DESCRIPTION	Sun Mon Tue Wed Thu Fri Sat					
CHORDS							
SCALES							
ARPEGGIOS							
SONGS							
LICKS/RIFFS							
OTHER							

TOPIC	DESCRIPTION	MINUTES						
		Sun	Mon	Tue	Wed	Thu	Fri	Sat
CHORDS								
SCALES								
ARPEGGIOS								
SONGS								
LICKS/RIFFS								
OTHER								

WEEK OF:

GOALS:

WEEK OF:									
GOALS:			MINUTES						
TOPIC	DESCRIPTION		Sun	Mon	Tue	Wed	Thu	Fri	Sat
CHORDS									
SCALES									
ARPEGGIOS									
SONGS									
LICKS/RIFFS									
OTHER									

WEEK OF:								
GOALS:				MINUTES				
TOPIC	**DESCRIPTION**	Sun	Mon	Tue	Wed	Thu	Fri	Sat
CHORDS								
SCALES								
ARPEGGIOS								
SONGS								
LICKS/RIFFS								
OTHER								

T
A
B

T
A
B

WEEK OF:								
GOALS:		MINUTES						
TOPIC	DESCRIPTION	Sun	Mon	Tue	Wed	Thu	Fri	Sat
CHORDS								
SCALES								
ARPEGGIOS								
SONGS								
LICKS/RIFFS								
OTHER								

TOPIC	DESCRIPTION	MINUTES						
		Sun	Mon	Tue	Wed	Thu	Fri	Sat
CHORDS								
SCALES								
ARPEGGIOS								
SONGS								
LICKS/RIFFS								
OTHER								

WEEK OF:

GOALS:

T
A
B

T
A
B

WEEK OF:									
GOALS:		MINUTES							
TOPIC	DESCRIPTION	Sun	Mon	Tue	Wed	Thu	Fri	Sat	
CHORDS									
SCALES									
ARPEGGIOS									
SONGS									
LICKS/RIFFS									
OTHER									

WEEK OF:									
GOALS:			MINUTES						
TOPIC	DESCRIPTION		Sun	Mon	Tue	Wed	Thu	Fri	Sat
CHORDS									
SCALES									
ARPEGGIOS									
SONGS									
LICKS/RIFFS									
OTHER									

WEEK OF:									
GOALS:			MINUTES						
TOPIC	DESCRIPTION		Sun	Mon	Tue	Wed	Thu	Fri	Sat
CHORDS									
SCALES									
ARPEGGIOS									
SONGS									
LICKS/RIFFS									
OTHER									

TOPIC	DESCRIPTION	MINUTES						
		Sun	Mon	Tue	Wed	Thu	Fri	Sat
CHORDS								
SCALES								
ARPEGGIOS								
SONGS								
LICKS/RIFFS								
OTHER								

WEEK OF:

GOALS:

WEEK OF:								
GOALS:		MINUTES						
TOPIC	DESCRIPTION	Sun	Mon	Tue	Wed	Thu	Fri	Sat
CHORDS								
SCALES								
ARPEGGIOS								
SONGS								
LICKS/RIFFS								
OTHER								

WEEK OF:									
GOALS:		MINUTES							
TOPIC	DESCRIPTION	Sun	Mon	Tue	Wed	Thu	Fri	Sat	
CHORDS									
SCALES									
ARPEGGIOS									
SONGS									
LICKS/RIFFS									
OTHER									

T
A
B

T
A
B

WEEK OF:									
GOALS:			MINUTES						
TOPIC	DESCRIPTION		Sun	Mon	Tue	Wed	Thu	Fri	Sat
CHORDS									
SCALES									
ARPEGGIOS									
SONGS									
LICKS/RIFFS									
OTHER									

WEEK OF:									
GOALS:			**MINUTES**						
TOPIC	**DESCRIPTION**		Sun	Mon	Tue	Wed	Thu	Fri	Sat
CHORDS									
SCALES									
ARPEGGIOS									
SONGS									
LICKS/RIFFS									
OTHER									

TAB

TAB

WEEK OF:								
GOALS:				MINUTES				
TOPIC	DESCRIPTION	Sun	Mon	Tue	Wed	Thu	Fri	Sat
CHORDS								
SCALES								
ARPEGGIOS								
SONGS								
LICKS/RIFFS								
OTHER								

WEEK OF:									
GOALS:		MINUTES							
TOPIC	DESCRIPTION	Sun	Mon	Tue	Wed	Thu	Fri	Sat	
CHORDS									
SCALES									
ARPEGGIOS									
SONGS									
LICKS/RIFFS									
OTHER									

WEEK OF:									
GOALS:			MINUTES						
TOPIC	DESCRIPTION		Sun	Mon	Tue	Wed	Thu	Fri	Sat
CHORDS									
SCALES									
ARPEGGIOS									
SONGS									
LICKS/RIFFS									
OTHER									

WEEK OF:										
GOALS:			MINUTES							
TOPIC	DESCRIPTION		Sun	Mon	Tue	Wed	Thu	Fri	Sat	
CHORDS										
SCALES										
ARPEGGIOS										
SONGS										
LICKS/RIFFS										
OTHER										

WEEK OF:								
GOALS:		MINUTES						
TOPIC	DESCRIPTION	Sun	Mon	Tue	Wed	Thu	Fri	Sat
CHORDS								
SCALES								
ARPEGGIOS								
SONGS								
LICKS/RIFFS								
OTHER								

WEEK OF:									
GOALS:			MINUTES						
TOPIC	DESCRIPTION		Sun	Mon	Tue	Wed	Thu	Fri	Sat
CHORDS									
SCALES									
ARPEGGIOS									
SONGS									
LICKS/RIFFS									
OTHER									

WEEK OF:								
GOALS:		MINUTES						
TOPIC	DESCRIPTION	Sun	Mon	Tue	Wed	Thu	Fri	Sat
CHORDS								
SCALES								
ARPEGGIOS								
SONGS								
LICKS/RIFFS								
OTHER								

WEEK OF:									
GOALS:				MINUTES					
TOPIC	DESCRIPTION	Sun	Mon	Tue	Wed	Thu	Fri	Sat
CHORDS								
SCALES								
ARPEGGIOS								
SONGS								
LICKS/RIFFS								
OTHER								

WEEK OF:									
GOALS:		MINUTES							
TOPIC	DESCRIPTION	Sun	Mon	Tue	Wed	Thu	Fri	Sat	
CHORDS									
SCALES									
ARPEGGIOS									
SONGS									
LICKS/RIFFS									
OTHER									

T
A
B

T
A
B

WEEK OF:									
GOALS:				MINUTES					
TOPIC	DESCRIPTION	Sun	Mon	Tue	Wed	Thu	Fri	Sat	
CHORDS									
SCALES									
ARPEGGIOS									
SONGS									
LICKS/RIFFS									
OTHER									

T
A
B

T
A
B

WEEK OF:								
GOALS:		MINUTES						
TOPIC	DESCRIPTION	Sun	Mon	Tue	Wed	Thu	Fri	Sat
CHORDS								
SCALES								
ARPEGGIOS								
SONGS								
LICKS/RIFFS								
OTHER								

WEEK OF:								
GOALS:			MINUTES					
TOPIC	DESCRIPTION	Sun	Mon	Tue	Wed	Thu	Fri	Sat
CHORDS								
SCALES								
ARPEGGIOS								
SONGS								
LICKS/RIFFS								
OTHER								

WEEK OF:								
GOALS:		MINUTES						
TOPIC	DESCRIPTION	Sun	Mon	Tue	Wed	Thu	Fri	Sat
CHORDS								
SCALES								
ARPEGGIOS								
SONGS								
LICKS/RIFFS								
OTHER								

WEEK OF:									
GOALS:			MINUTES						
TOPIC	DESCRIPTION		Sun	Mon	Tue	Wed	Thu	Fri	Sat
CHORDS									
SCALES									
ARPEGGIOS									
SONGS									
LICKS/RIFFS									
OTHER									

WEEK OF:									
GOALS:			MINUTES						
TOPIC	DESCRIPTION		Sun	Mon	Tue	Wed	Thu	Fri	Sat
CHORDS									
SCALES									
ARPEGGIOS									
SONGS									
LICKS/RIFFS									
OTHER									

WEEK OF:									
GOALS:		MINUTES							
TOPIC	DESCRIPTION	Sun	Mon	Tue	Wed	Thu	Fri	Sat
CHORDS								
SCALES								
ARPEGGIOS								
SONGS								
LICKS/RIFFS								
OTHER								

WEEK OF:								
GOALS:		MINUTES						
TOPIC	DESCRIPTION	Sun	Mon	Tue	Wed	Thu	Fri	Sat
CHORDS								
SCALES								
ARPEGGIOS								
SONGS								
LICKS/RIFFS								
OTHER								

WEEK OF:								
GOALS:			MINUTES					
TOPIC	DESCRIPTION	Sun	Mon	Tue	Wed	Thu	Fri	Sat
CHORDS								
SCALES								
ARPEGGIOS								
SONGS								
LICKS/RIFFS								
OTHER								

WEEK OF:									
GOALS:		MINUTES							
TOPIC	DESCRIPTION	Sun	Mon	Tue	Wed	Thu	Fri	Sat	
CHORDS									
SCALES									
ARPEGGIOS									
SONGS									
LICKS/RIFFS									
OTHER									

WEEK OF:									
GOALS:			MINUTES						
TOPIC	DESCRIPTION		Sun	Mon	Tue	Wed	Thu	Fri	Sat
CHORDS									
SCALES									
ARPEGGIOS									
SONGS									
LICKS/RIFFS									
OTHER									

WEEK OF:									
GOALS:		MINUTES							
TOPIC	DESCRIPTION	Sun	Mon	Tue	Wed	Thu	Fri	Sat
CHORDS								
SCALES								
ARPEGGIOS								
SONGS								
LICKS/RIFFS								
OTHER								

WEEK OF:								
GOALS:		MINUTES						
TOPIC	DESCRIPTION	Sun	Mon	Tue	Wed	Thu	Fri	Sat
CHORDS								
SCALES								
ARPEGGIOS								
SONGS								
LICKS/RIFFS								
OTHER								

WEEK OF:									
GOALS:			MINUTES						
TOPIC	DESCRIPTION		Sun	Mon	Tue	Wed	Thu	Fri	Sat
CHORDS									
SCALES									
ARPEGGIOS									
SONGS									
LICKS/RIFFS									
OTHER									

WEEK OF:										
GOALS:			MINUTES							
TOPIC	DESCRIPTION		Sun	Mon	Tue	Wed	Thu	Fri	Sat
CHORDS										
SCALES										
ARPEGGIOS										
SONGS										
LICKS/RIFFS										
OTHER										

TOPIC	DESCRIPTION	MINUTES						
		Sun	Mon	Tue	Wed	Thu	Fri	Sat
CHORDS								
SCALES								
ARPEGGIOS								
SONGS								
LICKS/RIFFS								
OTHER								

WEEK OF:

GOALS:

WEEK OF:									
GOALS:		MINUTES							
TOPIC	DESCRIPTION	Sun	Mon	Tue	Wed	Thu	Fri	Sat
CHORDS								
SCALES								
ARPEGGIOS								
SONGS								
LICKS/RIFFS								
OTHER								

WEEK OF:									
GOALS:			MINUTES						
TOPIC	DESCRIPTION	Sun	Mon	Tue	Wed	Thu	Fri	Sat
CHORDS								
SCALES								
ARPEGGIOS								
SONGS								
LICKS/RIFFS								
OTHER								

TOPIC	DESCRIPTION	MINUTES						
		Sun	Mon	Tue	Wed	Thu	Fri	Sat
CHORDS								
SCALES								
ARPEGGIOS								
SONGS								
LICKS/RIFFS								
OTHER								

WEEK OF:

GOALS:

WEEK OF:		MINUTES						
GOALS:								
TOPIC	DESCRIPTION	Sun	Mon	Tue	Wed	Thu	Fri	Sat
CHORDS								
SCALES								
ARPEGGIOS								
SONGS								
LICKS/RIFFS								
OTHER								

WEEK OF:									
GOALS:			MINUTES						
TOPIC	DESCRIPTION		Sun	Mon	Tue	Wed	Thu	Fri	Sat
CHORDS									
SCALES									
ARPEGGIOS									
SONGS									
LICKS/RIFFS									
OTHER									

T
A
B

T
A
B